50 Gourmet Mexican Recipes for Your Kitchen

By: Kelly Johnson

Table of Contents

- Cochinita Pibil Tacos
- Mole Poblano Enchiladas
- Chiles en Nogada
- Duck Carnitas Tostadas
- Shrimp Aguachile Verde
- Lobster Tamales with Chipotle Sauce
- Oaxacan Black Mole with Chicken
- Grilled Octopus with Salsa Verde
- Short Rib Barbacoa
- Poblano Cream Soup
- Mexican Street Corn Risotto
- Scallop Ceviche with Mango
- Carnitas Bao Buns
- Pozole Rojo with Pork
- Achiote Grilled Fish Tacos
- Roasted Poblano and Cheese Empanadas
- Sopes with Duck Confit
- Huitlacoche Quesadillas
- Beef Cheek Birria
- Smoky Mezcal Shrimp
- Pork Belly Tacos with Pickled Red Onions
- Squash Blossom Tamales
- Grilled Cactus Salad
- Tlayudas with Chorizo
- Mexican Chocolate Lava Cake
- Tamarind Glazed Ribs
- Stuffed Poblano Peppers with Walnut Sauce
- Cornbread with Jalapeño Honey Butter
- Avocado Gazpacho
- Pulled Chicken Tinga Tacos
- Duck Breast with Mole Amarillo
- Oaxaca-style Tlayuda Pizza
- Grilled Zucchini and Elote Salad
- Tamarind-Marinated Fish Filets
- Cactus and Cheese Stuffed Arepas

- Seared Scallops with Tomatillo Salsa
- Churro Cheesecake Bars
- Mexican Hot Chocolate Tart
- Roasted Tomato and Guajillo Salsa
- Slow-Cooked Pork Pozole Verde
- Chipotle Honey Glazed Salmon
- Poblano and Corn Fritters
- Guacamole with Pomegranate Seeds
- Mango Habanero Chicken Wings
- Chile Rellenos with Shrimp
- Black Bean and Goat Cheese Stuffed Peppers
- Pulled Pork Enchilada Casserole
- Spicy Jalapeño Margarita
- Hibiscus and Orange Agua Fresca
- Tequila Lime Cheesecake

Cochinita Pibil Tacos

Ingredients

For the Pork:

- 2 pounds (1 kg) pork shoulder or butt, cut into large chunks
- 2 tablespoons achiote paste
- 1/4 cup orange juice (freshly squeezed preferred)
- 2 tablespoons lime juice
- 4 garlic cloves, minced
- 1 teaspoon ground cumin
- 1 teaspoon dried oregano
- 1/2 teaspoon salt
- 1/4 teaspoon black pepper
- 1/2 cup chicken broth
- Banana leaves or aluminum foil (optional, for wrapping)

For the Pickled Red Onions:

- 1 medium red onion, thinly sliced
- 1/2 cup vinegar (white or apple cider)
- 1/4 cup water
- 1 teaspoon sugar
- 1/2 teaspoon salt

To Assemble:

- Corn tortillas, warmed
- Fresh cilantro, chopped
- Lime wedges
- Optional: Crumbled queso fresco, sliced avocado, or salsa of your choice

Instructions

1. **Prepare the Marinade:**
   In a blender or small bowl, combine achiote paste, orange juice, lime juice, garlic, cumin, oregano, salt, and pepper. Blend or whisk until smooth.
2. **Marinate the Pork:**
   Place pork chunks in a large bowl or zip-top bag. Pour the marinade over the

pork, ensuring all pieces are coated. Cover and refrigerate for at least 4 hours or overnight for best flavor.

3. **Cook the Pork:**
   Preheat the oven to 300°F (150°C).
   Line a baking dish with banana leaves or foil if using. Add the pork and pour in the chicken broth. Wrap tightly with the leaves or cover with foil to seal.
   Cook in the oven for 3–4 hours until the pork is tender and easy to shred.

4. **Make the Pickled Onions:**
   While the pork cooks, combine vinegar, water, sugar, and salt in a small saucepan. Bring to a simmer.
   Pour the hot mixture over the sliced onions in a bowl. Let them sit for at least 30 minutes, or until ready to serve.

5. **Shred the Pork:**
   Remove the pork from the oven and shred with two forks. Toss it in the cooking juices to keep it moist and flavorful.

6. **Assemble the Tacos:**
   Place a generous portion of shredded pork on a warm tortilla. Top with pickled onions, cilantro, and any additional toppings. Serve with lime wedges for a burst of citrus.

Mole Poblano Enchiladas

Ingredients:

For the Mole Poblano Sauce:

- 2 dried ancho chilies
- 2 dried pasilla chilies
- 1 dried mulato chili (optional)
- 1/4 cup sesame seeds
- 1/4 cup almonds or peanuts
- 1/4 cup pumpkin seeds (pepitas)
- 1 small onion, chopped
- 2 garlic cloves, minced
- 1 medium tomato, chopped
- 1/2 teaspoon ground cinnamon
- 1/2 teaspoon ground cumin
- 1/4 teaspoon ground cloves
- 2 tablespoons dark chocolate (or Mexican chocolate, if available)
- 1/4 cup raisins or dried apricots
- 2 cups chicken or vegetable broth
- 2 tablespoons vegetable oil
- Salt to taste
- 1/2 tablespoon sugar (optional, depending on sweetness preference)

For the Enchiladas:

- 10-12 corn tortillas
- 2 cups cooked chicken, shredded (or beef, pork, or vegetables for a vegetarian option)
- 1 cup grated Oaxaca cheese (or any soft, melty cheese like Monterey Jack)
- 1/2 cup finely chopped onion (optional, for garnish)
- Fresh cilantro (optional, for garnish)
- Sour cream (optional, for serving)
- Lime wedges (optional, for serving)

Instructions:

1. **Make the Mole Poblano Sauce:**
   - **Toast the dried chilies:** Remove the stems and seeds from the dried ancho, pasilla, and mulato chilies. Toast them in a dry skillet over medium heat

for about 2 minutes until fragrant, being careful not to burn them. Once toasted, cover with hot water and let them soak for about 15 minutes, until softened.
    - **Blend the chilies:** Drain the chilies and place them in a blender or food processor. Add the sesame seeds, almonds, pumpkin seeds, chopped onion, garlic, tomato, cinnamon, cumin, cloves, chocolate, raisins, and a pinch of salt. Pour in about 1 cup of chicken broth and blend until smooth.
    - **Cook the mole:** Heat the vegetable oil in a saucepan over medium heat. Pour the mole paste into the pan and cook, stirring frequently, for about 5-7 minutes to bring out the flavors. Add the remaining chicken broth and stir. Simmer for another 15-20 minutes, allowing the sauce to thicken and the flavors to meld. Taste and adjust seasoning with salt and sugar if needed. If the mole is too thick, you can add a little more broth to reach your desired consistency.
2. **Prepare the Enchiladas:**
    - **Warm the tortillas:** Lightly warm the tortillas in a dry skillet or microwave them for a few seconds to make them more pliable.
    - **Assemble the enchiladas:** Place a small amount of shredded chicken (or your choice of filling) in the center of each tortilla. Roll up the tortillas tightly around the filling and place them seam side down in a baking dish.
    - **Cover with mole sauce:** Pour the mole poblano sauce generously over the enchiladas, ensuring each one is well-coated.
    - **Top with cheese:** Sprinkle the grated Oaxaca cheese over the mole-covered enchiladas.
3. **Bake and Serve:**
    - Preheat your oven to 350°F (175°C). Bake the enchiladas for about 20-25 minutes, or until the cheese is melted and bubbly.
    - **Garnish:** Top with chopped onion, fresh cilantro, and a dollop of sour cream if desired. Serve with lime wedges on the side.

Chiles en Nogada

Ingredients:

For the Poblano Peppers:

- 6 large poblano peppers
- 1 tablespoon vegetable oil

For the Picadillo Filling:

- 1 tablespoon vegetable oil
- 1 lb ground pork (or a mix of pork and beef)
- 1 medium onion, chopped
- 2 garlic cloves, minced
- 1 medium tomato, chopped
- 1/2 cup chopped dried fruit (raisins, apricots, or peaches)
- 1/4 cup almonds, chopped
- 1/4 cup candied or fresh plantains, chopped (optional)
- 1/2 teaspoon ground cinnamon
- 1/4 teaspoon ground cloves
- 1/2 teaspoon cumin
- Salt and pepper to taste
- 1/4 cup fresh parsley, chopped
- 1/4 cup pomegranate seeds (for garnish)

For the Nogada Sauce:

- 1 cup walnuts, soaked in water for 1-2 hours
- 1/2 cup milk
- 1/4 cup heavy cream
- 1 tablespoon sugar
- 1 tablespoon cinnamon
- Pinch of salt

Instructions:

1. **Roast the Poblano Peppers:** Char the poblano peppers directly over a flame or in a broiler until the skins are blackened. Place the peppers in a plastic bag or bowl covered with a towel to steam for about 10 minutes. Peel off the skins, remove the seeds, and set aside.

2. **Prepare the Picadillo Filling:** Heat vegetable oil in a pan over medium heat. Add the ground pork and cook until browned. Add onion and garlic and cook until soft. Stir in tomato, dried fruit, almonds, plantains (if using), cinnamon, cloves, and cumin. Cook for another 5-7 minutes, allowing the flavors to meld. Season with salt and pepper and stir in fresh parsley. Set aside to cool.
3. **Make the Nogada Sauce:** In a blender, combine the soaked walnuts, milk, cream, sugar, cinnamon, and salt. Blend until smooth. Add more milk if the sauce is too thick.
4. **Stuff the Peppers:** Gently stuff the roasted poblano peppers with the picadillo filling. Arrange them on a plate.
5. **Serve:** Pour the nogada sauce over the stuffed peppers. Garnish with pomegranate seeds and fresh parsley.

Duck Carnitas Tostadas

Ingredients:

- 2 duck breasts, skin on
- 2 tablespoons vegetable oil
- 1/2 onion, chopped
- 2 garlic cloves, minced
- 1 orange, juiced
- 1 teaspoon cumin
- 1 teaspoon smoked paprika
- 1/2 teaspoon ground cloves
- 1/2 teaspoon cinnamon
- Salt and pepper to taste
- 8 tostada shells
- 1 cup shredded lettuce
- 1/2 cup fresh salsa
- 1/2 cup crumbled queso fresco
- Lime wedges (for serving)

Instructions:

1. **Prepare the Duck:** Score the skin of the duck breasts and season with salt, pepper, cumin, paprika, cloves, and cinnamon.
2. **Cook the Duck:** Heat vegetable oil in a skillet over medium-high heat. Place the duck breasts skin-side down and sear for about 5-6 minutes. Flip and cook for an additional 4-5 minutes. Remove from heat and let rest. Shred the duck meat.
3. **Prepare the Carnitas:** In the same skillet, sauté the chopped onion and garlic until soft. Add the orange juice and season with more salt and pepper. Toss in the shredded duck and cook, stirring occasionally, until the duck is crispy and caramelized.
4. **Assemble the Tostadas:** Top the tostada shells with shredded lettuce. Spoon the duck carnitas on top. Add salsa, crumbled queso fresco, and a squeeze of lime.
5. **Serve:** Garnish with fresh cilantro and serve with extra lime wedges on the side.

Shrimp Aguachile Verde

Ingredients:

- 1 lb raw shrimp, peeled and deveined
- 1 cucumber, thinly sliced
- 1/2 red onion, thinly sliced
- 2-3 serrano peppers, stems removed
- 1/2 cup fresh cilantro
- 1/4 cup lime juice (about 4 limes)
- 1/4 cup lemon juice (about 2 lemons)
- 1/4 cup orange juice
- 1 tablespoon olive oil
- Salt to taste
- Sliced avocado (for garnish)
- Fresh cilantro leaves (for garnish)

Instructions:

1. **Prepare the Shrimp:** Slice the shrimp into thin rounds and place them in a glass or ceramic bowl.
2. **Make the Aguachile Marinade:** In a blender, combine serrano peppers, cilantro, lime juice, lemon juice, orange juice, olive oil, and salt. Blend until smooth.
3. **Marinate the Shrimp:** Pour the aguachile marinade over the shrimp and stir to coat. Let the shrimp marinate for about 15-20 minutes, allowing the citric acid to "cook" the shrimp.
4. **Assemble the Dish:** Arrange the marinated shrimp on a plate, and top with thinly sliced cucumber, onion, and avocado.
5. **Serve:** Garnish with fresh cilantro leaves and serve immediately.

Lobster Tamales with Chipotle Sauce

Ingredients:

For the Tamales:

- 1 lb lobster meat, cooked and chopped
- 2 cups masa harina (corn dough)
- 1 cup chicken broth
- 1/2 cup vegetable oil or melted butter
- 1 teaspoon baking powder
- 1 teaspoon salt
- 10-12 dried corn husks, soaked in warm water

For the Chipotle Sauce:

- 2 chipotle peppers in adobo sauce
- 1 cup tomato sauce
- 1/4 cup chicken broth
- 2 cloves garlic, minced
- 1 tablespoon vegetable oil
- Salt and pepper to taste

Instructions:

1. **Make the Tamales:**
    - In a large bowl, mix the masa harina, baking powder, salt, vegetable oil, and chicken broth. Knead the dough until soft and pliable. If it feels dry, add more chicken broth until the dough reaches a smooth consistency.
    - Gently fold in the cooked lobster meat.
    - Take a corn husk, spread a small amount of masa dough on it, and form a log shape. Fold the sides of the husk over the dough, then fold up the bottom of the husk to seal the tamale.
    - Steam the tamales for about 1-1.5 hours until the masa is fully cooked and releases easily from the husk.
2. **Make the Chipotle Sauce:**
    - In a saucepan, heat oil over medium heat. Add the garlic and sauté until fragrant.
    - Add the chipotle peppers, tomato sauce, chicken broth, salt, and pepper. Simmer for 10-15 minutes until the sauce thickens slightly.

- Puree the sauce with an immersion blender or regular blender until smooth.
3. **Serve:**
    - Plate the tamales and drizzle with chipotle sauce. Serve warm.

Oaxacan Black Mole with Chicken

Ingredients:

For the Mole:

- 4 dried pasilla chilies
- 4 dried mulato chilies
- 1 dried ancho chili
- 2 tablespoons sesame seeds
- 1/4 cup almonds
- 1/4 cup peanuts
- 1/4 cup pumpkin seeds
- 2 tablespoons dark chocolate
- 1/2 teaspoon ground cinnamon
- 1 teaspoon ground cumin
- 2 cloves garlic, minced
- 1 small onion, chopped
- 2 cups chicken broth
- 1 tablespoon vegetable oil
- Salt to taste

For the Chicken:

- 4 chicken breasts, cooked and shredded
- 1 tablespoon vegetable oil
- Salt and pepper to taste

Instructions:

1. **Prepare the Mole:**
    - Toast the dried chilies in a skillet over medium heat until fragrant. Remove stems and seeds, then soak in hot water for 15 minutes to soften.
    - Blend the chilies with sesame seeds, almonds, peanuts, pumpkin seeds, dark chocolate, cinnamon, cumin, garlic, onion, and chicken broth. Blend until smooth.
    - Heat oil in a saucepan over medium heat, then pour in the mole mixture. Simmer for 20-25 minutes, adjusting salt as needed.
2. **Prepare the Chicken:**
    - Heat oil in a pan over medium heat. Add the shredded chicken, season with salt and pepper, and cook for 5-7 minutes until heated through.

3. **Serve:**
    - Serve the shredded chicken topped with the Oaxacan black mole sauce. Garnish with sesame seeds if desired.

Grilled Octopus with Salsa Verde

Ingredients:

- 2 lbs octopus, cleaned and tenderized
- 2 tablespoons olive oil
- 1 lemon, juiced
- Salt and pepper to taste
- 1 cup salsa verde (prepared or homemade)

Instructions:

1. **Prepare the Octopus:**
     - Bring a large pot of salted water to a boil. Add the octopus and cook for about 40-45 minutes until tender.
     - Once tender, remove from water, brush with olive oil, and season with salt, pepper, and lemon juice.
2. **Grill the Octopus:**
     - Preheat the grill to medium-high heat.
     - Grill the octopus for 3-4 minutes per side, until charred and slightly crispy on the edges.
3. **Serve:**
     - Slice the octopus and serve with salsa verde.

Short Rib Barbacoa

Ingredients:

- 3 lbs beef short ribs
- 2 dried ancho chilies
- 2 dried guajillo chilies
- 1 medium onion, chopped
- 4 cloves garlic, minced
- 1 tablespoon cumin
- 1 tablespoon oregano
- 1/4 cup apple cider vinegar
- 2 cups beef broth
- Salt and pepper to taste

Instructions:

1. **Prepare the Short Ribs:**
    - Season the short ribs with salt, pepper, cumin, and oregano. Heat oil in a large pot and sear the short ribs on all sides.
    - Remove the ribs and set aside.
2. **Make the Barbacoa Sauce:**
    - Toast the dried chilies in a hot skillet until fragrant, then remove stems and seeds.
    - Blend the chilies, garlic, onion, apple cider vinegar, and beef broth until smooth.
3. **Cook the Barbacoa:**
    - Return the short ribs to the pot and pour in the barbacoa sauce. Cover and simmer for 2.5-3 hours, until the meat is tender and falling off the bone.
4. **Serve:**
    - Shred the beef and serve with tortillas or rice.

Poblano Cream Soup

Ingredients:

- 2 large poblano peppers
- 1 tablespoon vegetable oil
- 1 onion, chopped
- 2 garlic cloves, minced
- 1 large potato, peeled and chopped
- 4 cups vegetable or chicken broth
- 1 cup heavy cream
- Salt and pepper to taste

Instructions:

1. **Roast the Poblanos:**
    - Char the poblanos under a broiler or over an open flame. Peel off the skins, remove seeds, and set aside.
2. **Make the Soup:**
    - Heat oil in a pot over medium heat. Add onion and garlic and sauté until soft.
    - Add the chopped potato, roasted poblano peppers, broth, and salt. Bring to a simmer and cook for 15-20 minutes.
    - Blend until smooth, then stir in heavy cream.
3. **Serve:**
    - Adjust seasoning and serve hot.

Mexican Street Corn Risotto

Ingredients:

- 1 cup Arborio rice
- 2 tablespoons butter
- 1 tablespoon olive oil
- 1/2 cup white wine
- 4 cups chicken broth, warmed
- 2 cups corn kernels (fresh or frozen)
- 1/2 cup cotija cheese, crumbled
- 1/2 teaspoon chili powder
- Salt and pepper to taste
- Fresh cilantro for garnish

Instructions:

1. **Prepare the Risotto:**
   - In a pan, heat oil and butter. Add the rice and toast it for 2-3 minutes.
   - Add the wine and let it evaporate. Gradually add warm broth, one ladle at a time, stirring frequently until the liquid is absorbed.
2. **Add the Corn:**
   - Stir in the corn kernels and continue to cook until the rice is tender and creamy.
3. **Finish the Dish:**
   - Stir in cotija cheese, chili powder, salt, and pepper.
4. **Serve:**
   - Garnish with fresh cilantro and extra cotija cheese.

Scallop Ceviche with Mango

Ingredients:

- 1 lb fresh scallops, thinly sliced
- 1 ripe mango, diced
- 1 small red onion, thinly sliced
- 1-2 serrano chilies, minced
- 1/4 cup fresh cilantro, chopped
- 1/4 cup lime juice
- Salt to taste

Instructions:

1. **Prepare the Ceviche:**
    - In a bowl, combine scallops, mango, onion, chilies, and cilantro. Pour lime juice over the mixture and stir gently.
2. **Marinate:**
    - Refrigerate for 15-20 minutes, allowing the scallops to "cook" in the lime juice.
3. **Serve:**
    - Season with salt and serve chilled.

Carnitas Bao Buns

Ingredients:

- 2 lbs pork shoulder, cut into chunks
- 1 tablespoon vegetable oil
- 1 onion, chopped
- 4 cloves garlic, minced
- 1 tablespoon cumin
- 1 tablespoon oregano
- 1/4 cup orange juice
- 1/4 cup chicken broth
- Salt and pepper to taste
- 10-12 bao buns, steamed

Instructions:

1. **Cook the Carnitas:**
   - Heat oil in a large pot and brown the pork chunks on all sides.
   - Add onion, garlic, cumin, oregano, orange juice, chicken broth, salt, and pepper. Cover and simmer for 2.5-3 hours, until the pork is tender and easily shreds.
2. **Shred the Pork:**
   - Shred the pork using two forks, discarding any fat.
3. **Assemble the Bao Buns:**
   - Fill the steamed bao buns with carnitas and serve with your favorite toppings such as pickled onions, cilantro, and a squeeze of lime.

Pozole Rojo with Pork

Ingredients:

- 2 lbs pork shoulder, cut into chunks
- 2 tablespoons vegetable oil
- 1 large onion, quartered
- 4 cloves garlic, minced
- 3 dried guajillo chilies, seeds removed
- 2 dried ancho chilies, seeds removed
- 1 can (15 oz) hominy, drained
- 6 cups chicken broth
- 1 teaspoon cumin
- 1 teaspoon oregano
- Salt to taste
- 1/2 teaspoon ground chili powder (optional, for extra heat)

Garnishes:

- Sliced radishes
- Chopped cilantro
- Lime wedges
- Shredded cabbage
- Oregano

Instructions:

1. **Prepare the Pork:**
   - In a large pot, heat vegetable oil over medium-high heat. Brown the pork shoulder chunks in batches and remove them from the pot.
   - Add the onion and garlic to the same pot and sauté until softened.
2. **Make the Red Sauce:**
   - Toast the dried chilies lightly in a dry skillet until fragrant, then soak them in hot water for 15 minutes.
   - Blend the soaked chilies with a bit of broth until smooth. Add the cumin, oregano, and optional chili powder.
3. **Cook the Pozole:**
   - Return the browned pork to the pot, add the red chili sauce, hominy, and chicken broth. Bring to a boil, then lower the heat to a simmer.
   - Cook for 2-2.5 hours, until the pork is tender and the flavors have melded. Season with salt to taste.
4. **Serve:**

- Serve the pozole hot with your choice of garnishes such as radishes, cilantro, lime, and shredded cabbage.

Achiote Grilled Fish Tacos

Ingredients:

- 1 lb white fish fillets (like tilapia or cod)
- 1/4 cup achiote paste
- 2 tablespoons orange juice
- 1 tablespoon lime juice
- 1 teaspoon garlic powder
- 1 teaspoon ground cumin
- Salt and pepper to taste
- 8 small corn tortillas

For the Toppings:

- Sliced cabbage
- Avocado slices
- Fresh cilantro
- Lime wedges

Instructions:

1. **Marinate the Fish:**
    - In a bowl, combine achiote paste, orange juice, lime juice, garlic powder, cumin, salt, and pepper. Mix to form a marinade.
    - Coat the fish fillets with the marinade and let them sit for at least 30 minutes.
2. **Grill the Fish:**
    - Preheat the grill or a grill pan over medium-high heat. Grill the fish for 3-4 minutes per side, or until cooked through and flakey.
3. **Assemble the Tacos:**
    - Warm the corn tortillas on the grill for 30 seconds on each side.
    - Flake the grilled fish into the tortillas and top with sliced cabbage, avocado, fresh cilantro, and a squeeze of lime.

Roasted Poblano and Cheese Empanadas

Ingredients:

- 2 large poblano peppers
- 1 tablespoon olive oil
- 1 small onion, chopped
- 2 cups shredded cheese (such as Oaxaca or Monterey Jack)
- 1 tablespoon chopped fresh cilantro
- 1 package of empanada dough discs (about 10-12)
- 1 egg (for egg wash)
- Salt and pepper to taste

Instructions:

1. **Roast the Poblanos:**
    - Char the poblanos over an open flame or under the broiler. Peel off the skins, remove the seeds, and chop the peppers.
2. **Prepare the Filling:**
    - Heat olive oil in a pan over medium heat. Sauté the chopped onion until softened, then add the roasted poblano peppers. Cook for 5 minutes, then remove from heat.
    - Mix the poblano mixture with the shredded cheese and cilantro. Season with salt and pepper.
3. **Assemble the Empanadas:**
    - Preheat the oven to 375°F (190°C). Place a spoonful of filling in the center of each empanada disc.
    - Fold the disc in half and crimp the edges with a fork to seal. Brush each empanada with a beaten egg.
4. **Bake:**
    - Place the empanadas on a baking sheet and bake for 20-25 minutes or until golden brown.

Sopes with Duck Confit

Ingredients:

- 4 sopes (thick corn masa cakes)
- 2 duck legs, confit
- 1 tablespoon vegetable oil
- 1/2 cup refried beans
- 1/4 cup crumbled queso fresco
- 1/4 cup fresh cilantro, chopped
- 1/2 red onion, thinly sliced
- Salsa (your favorite type)

Instructions:

1. **Prepare the Duck Confit:**
    - Shred the duck confit meat from the bone and discard the skin. Sauté the shredded meat in vegetable oil over medium heat until crispy, about 5-7 minutes.
2. **Assemble the Sopes:**
    - Heat the sopes in a dry pan until slightly crispy.
    - Spread a layer of refried beans on each sope. Top with the crispy duck confit, crumbled queso fresco, sliced onions, and fresh cilantro.
3. **Serve:**
    - Drizzle with salsa and serve immediately.

Huitlacoche Quesadillas

Ingredients:

- 1 cup huitlacoche (corn truffles), fresh or canned
- 1 tablespoon butter
- 1/2 cup onion, finely chopped
- 1 cup shredded cheese (such as Oaxaca or Chihuahua)
- 4 flour tortillas
- Salt and pepper to taste

Instructions:

1. **Prepare the Huitlacoche:**
    - In a pan, melt the butter over medium heat. Sauté the onion until softened, then add the huitlacoche and cook for 5-7 minutes, seasoning with salt and pepper.
2. **Assemble the Quesadillas:**
    - Place a flour tortilla on a griddle and sprinkle half of the cheese on top. Add half of the huitlacoche mixture and top with the remaining cheese. Place another tortilla on top.
    - Cook each quesadilla for 2-3 minutes per side, until golden brown and the cheese has melted.
3. **Serve:**
    - Slice the quesadillas into wedges and serve hot.

Beef Cheek Birria

Ingredients:

- 2 lbs beef cheeks, trimmed and cut into chunks
- 2 dried guajillo chilies
- 2 dried pasilla chilies
- 2 dried ancho chilies
- 4 cloves garlic
- 1 onion, quartered
- 1 cinnamon stick
- 1 teaspoon cumin
- 2 cups beef broth
- Salt to taste
- 1 tablespoon vegetable oil

Instructions:

1. **Prepare the Chilies:**
    - Toast the dried chilies in a skillet until fragrant. Remove the stems and seeds, then soak them in hot water for 20 minutes.
2. **Make the Sauce:**
    - Blend the soaked chilies, garlic, onion, cumin, and beef broth until smooth.
3. **Cook the Birria:**
    - Heat oil in a large pot over medium heat and brown the beef cheeks in batches. Add the chili sauce, cinnamon stick, and enough beef broth to cover the meat.
    - Simmer for 3-4 hours, or until the beef is tender and shreds easily.
4. **Serve:**
    - Shred the beef and serve with warm tortillas and a side of the rich broth for dipping.

Smoky Mezcal Shrimp

Ingredients:

- 1 lb large shrimp, peeled and deveined
- 1/4 cup mezcal
- 2 tablespoons olive oil
- 1 tablespoon smoked paprika
- 1 teaspoon garlic powder
- Salt and pepper to taste
- 1 tablespoon fresh lime juice
- Fresh cilantro for garnish

Instructions:

1. **Marinate the Shrimp:**
    - In a bowl, combine mezcal, olive oil, smoked paprika, garlic powder, salt, and pepper. Add the shrimp and marinate for 15-20 minutes.
2. **Cook the Shrimp:**
    - Heat a grill pan or skillet over medium-high heat. Cook the shrimp for 2-3 minutes per side until pink and cooked through.
3. **Serve:**
    - Garnish with lime juice and fresh cilantro. Serve immediately.

Pork Belly Tacos with Pickled Red Onions

Ingredients:

- 1 lb pork belly, skin removed and cut into 1-inch cubes
- 1 tablespoon vegetable oil
- 1 teaspoon cumin
- 1 teaspoon chili powder
- Salt and pepper to taste
- 8 small corn tortillas
- 1/2 red onion, thinly sliced
- 1/4 cup vinegar
- 1 tablespoon sugar
- 1/4 teaspoon salt

Instructions:

1. **Prepare the Pork Belly:**
   - Heat oil in a large skillet over medium-high heat. Season the pork belly cubes with cumin, chili powder, salt, and pepper.
   - Cook the pork belly for 10-15 minutes, until crispy on the outside and tender on the inside.
2. **Pickle the Onions:**
   - In a small bowl, combine the vinegar, sugar, and salt. Add the red onions and let them sit for 10 minutes.
3. **Assemble the Tacos:**
   - Warm the tortillas and fill them with the crispy pork belly and pickled red onions.
4. **Serve:**
   - Serve the tacos with a squeeze of lime and your favorite salsa.

Squash Blossom Tamales

Ingredients:

- 2 cups masa harina
- 1 cup chicken or vegetable broth
- 1/2 cup vegetable oil
- 1 teaspoon baking powder
- 1 teaspoon salt
- 2 cups squash blossoms, cleaned and chopped
- 1/2 cup crumbled queso fresco
- 12 corn husks, soaked in warm water

Instructions:

1. **Prepare the Masa:**
   - In a large bowl, combine masa harina, baking powder, and salt. Slowly add broth and vegetable oil, stirring until smooth.
2. **Make the Filling:**
   - In a separate bowl, mix the chopped squash blossoms with the crumbled queso fresco.
3. **Assemble the Tamales:**
   - Spread a thin layer of masa on the soaked corn husks, leaving space at the edges. Add a spoonful of the squash blossom mixture in the center.
   - Fold the sides of the husk inwards, then fold up the bottom of the husk to secure the tamale.
4. **Steam the Tamales:**
   - Arrange the tamales in a steamer and steam for 1 to 1.5 hours, checking periodically to ensure they are fully cooked.

Grilled Cactus Salad

Ingredients:

- 2 cactus pads (nopales), cleaned and sliced into strips
- 1 tablespoon olive oil
- Salt and pepper to taste
- 1/4 cup red onion, finely chopped
- 1/4 cup fresh cilantro, chopped
- 1/2 cup cherry tomatoes, halved
- 1 tablespoon lime juice
- 1 tablespoon olive oil

Instructions:

1. **Grill the Cactus:**
   - Brush the cactus strips with olive oil, season with salt and pepper, and grill on medium-high heat for 2-3 minutes per side until tender and slightly charred.
2. **Prepare the Salad:**
   - In a large bowl, combine the grilled cactus, red onion, cilantro, and cherry tomatoes.
3. **Dress the Salad:**
   - Drizzle with lime juice and olive oil, toss gently, and serve immediately.

Tlayudas with Chorizo

Ingredients:

- 4 large flour tortillas
- 1 lb fresh chorizo sausage, casing removed
- 1/2 cup refried black beans
- 1 cup Oaxaca cheese, shredded
- 1/2 cup lettuce, shredded
- 1 tomato, sliced
- 1/4 cup pickled red onions
- Salsa (optional)

Instructions:

1. **Cook the Chorizo:**
    - In a pan, cook the chorizo over medium heat until browned and crispy, breaking it up with a spoon as it cooks.
2. **Prepare the Tlayuda Base:**
    - Heat the flour tortillas on a griddle or skillet until crispy, about 2 minutes on each side.
3. **Assemble the Tlayudas:**
    - Spread a thin layer of refried black beans on each crispy tortilla. Add the cooked chorizo, shredded cheese, lettuce, tomato slices, and pickled red onions.
4. **Serve:**
    - Serve with salsa on the side and enjoy.

Mexican Chocolate Lava Cake

Ingredients:

- 1/2 cup unsweetened Mexican chocolate, chopped
- 1/2 cup unsalted butter
- 1 cup powdered sugar
- 2 large eggs
- 2 large egg yolks
- 1 teaspoon vanilla extract
- 1/2 cup all-purpose flour
- 1/4 teaspoon cinnamon
- Pinch of salt

Instructions:

1. **Prepare the Batter:**
    - Melt the Mexican chocolate and butter together in a heatproof bowl over simmering water. Let it cool slightly.
    - Whisk in the powdered sugar, eggs, egg yolks, and vanilla. Add the flour, cinnamon, and salt, and mix until smooth.
2. **Bake the Lava Cakes:**
    - Grease four ramekins and divide the batter evenly among them. Place a piece of chocolate in the center of each ramekin.
    - Bake at 425°F (220°C) for 12-14 minutes, or until the edges are set but the center is still soft.
3. **Serve:**
    - Let the cakes cool for a minute, then invert onto plates. Serve with whipped cream or vanilla ice cream.

Tamarind Glazed Ribs

Ingredients:

- 2 racks of baby back ribs
- Salt and pepper to taste
- 1/2 cup tamarind paste
- 1/4 cup brown sugar
- 1/4 cup soy sauce
- 1/4 cup lime juice
- 1/4 teaspoon chili powder

Instructions:

1. **Prepare the Ribs:**
    - Preheat your oven to 300°F (150°C). Season the ribs with salt and pepper. Place them on a baking sheet lined with foil and bake for 2.5 hours.
2. **Make the Tamarind Glaze:**
    - In a saucepan, combine tamarind paste, brown sugar, soy sauce, lime juice, and chili powder. Simmer over medium heat for 10-15 minutes until thickened.
3. **Glaze and Grill the Ribs:**
    - Brush the tamarind glaze on the ribs and grill over medium heat for 5-10 minutes, basting with more glaze until caramelized.
4. **Serve:**
    - Serve the ribs with additional tamarind glaze on the side.

Stuffed Poblano Peppers with Walnut Sauce

Ingredients:

- 4 large poblano peppers
- 1 cup cooked quinoa or rice
- 1/2 cup cooked ground beef or turkey
- 1/2 cup cheese (cheddar or Oaxaca), shredded
- 1/4 cup fresh cilantro, chopped
- 1/4 cup walnuts, chopped
- 1/4 cup heavy cream
- 1 tablespoon olive oil
- Salt and pepper to taste

Instructions:

1. **Roast the Poblanos:**
    - Roast the poblano peppers over an open flame or under the broiler until charred. Peel off the skins and remove the seeds.
2. **Prepare the Filling:**
    - In a bowl, mix the cooked quinoa or rice, ground meat, cheese, and cilantro. Season with salt and pepper.
3. **Make the Walnut Sauce:**
    - In a blender, combine walnuts, heavy cream, and olive oil. Blend until smooth.
4. **Stuff and Bake:**
    - Stuff each roasted poblano with the quinoa mixture. Place in a baking dish and pour the walnut sauce over the top. Bake at 375°F (190°C) for 20-25 minutes until heated through.

Cornbread with Jalapeño Honey Butter

Ingredients:

- 1 cup cornmeal
- 1 cup all-purpose flour
- 1 tablespoon baking powder
- 1/2 cup sugar
- 1 cup milk
- 2 large eggs
- 1/4 cup unsalted butter, melted
- 1 cup shredded cheddar cheese
- 2 fresh jalapeños, diced

For the Jalapeño Honey Butter:

- 1/2 cup unsalted butter, softened
- 2 tablespoons honey
- 1 fresh jalapeño, minced

Instructions:

1. **Prepare the Cornbread:**
   - Preheat the oven to 375°F (190°C). In a large bowl, mix cornmeal, flour, baking powder, and sugar. Add milk, eggs, and melted butter, then stir in shredded cheese and jalapeños.
   - Pour the batter into a greased baking dish and bake for 25-30 minutes, until golden brown.
2. **Make the Jalapeño Honey Butter:**
   - In a small bowl, combine softened butter, honey, and minced jalapeño. Mix until smooth.
3. **Serve:**
   - Serve the cornbread warm with a dollop of jalapeño honey butter.

Avocado Gazpacho

Ingredients:

- 2 ripe avocados, peeled and pitted
- 2 cups cucumber, peeled and chopped
- 1/2 cup red onion, chopped
- 1 clove garlic, minced
- 1/4 cup lime juice
- 2 cups cold water
- 1 tablespoon olive oil
- Salt and pepper to taste
- Fresh cilantro for garnish

Instructions:

1. **Blend the Soup:**
   - In a blender, combine avocados, cucumber, onion, garlic, lime juice, cold water, olive oil, salt, and pepper. Blend until smooth.
2. **Chill:**
   - Refrigerate the gazpacho for at least 1 hour before serving.
3. **Serve:**
   - Garnish with fresh cilantro and serve cold.

Pulled Chicken Tinga Tacos

Ingredients:

- 2 lbs chicken breast
- 2 tablespoons olive oil
- 1 onion, thinly sliced
- 3 cloves garlic, minced
- 2 dried guajillo chilies
- 2 tomatoes, diced
- 1 teaspoon ground cumin
- 1/2 teaspoon chili powder
- Salt and pepper to taste
- 12 corn tortillas
- Fresh cilantro for garnish
- Lime wedges for serving

Instructions:

1. **Cook the Chicken:**
    - In a large pot, cook the chicken in salted water until tender (about 25-30 minutes). Shred the chicken once it's cool enough to handle.
2. **Prepare the Tinga Sauce:**
    - In a pan, heat olive oil and sauté onions and garlic until softened. Add the chopped tomatoes, cumin, chili powder, and the guajillo chilies (rehydrated and chopped). Simmer for 10-15 minutes until the sauce thickens.
3. **Assemble the Tacos:**
    - Toss the shredded chicken in the tinga sauce and warm the corn tortillas. Fill each tortilla with the chicken mixture.
4. **Serve:**
    - Garnish with fresh cilantro and serve with lime wedges.

Duck Breast with Mole Amarillo

Ingredients:

- 2 duck breasts, skin-on
- Salt and pepper to taste
- 1/2 cup Mole Amarillo (store-bought or homemade)
- 1 tablespoon vegetable oil

Instructions:

1. **Prepare the Duck Breasts:**
    - Score the skin of the duck breasts and season both sides with salt and pepper.
2. **Cook the Duck:**
    - Heat vegetable oil in a skillet over medium heat. Place the duck breasts skin-side down and cook for 6-8 minutes until the skin is crispy and golden.
    - Flip the duck and cook for an additional 4-5 minutes for medium-rare. Adjust cooking time depending on desired doneness.
    - Remove from the skillet and let rest for 5 minutes before slicing.
3. **Serve:**
    - Spoon warm Mole Amarillo over the duck breast slices and serve.

Oaxaca-style Tlayuda Pizza

Ingredients:

- 4 large flour tortillas
- 1/2 cup refried black beans
- 1 cup Oaxaca cheese, shredded
- 1/2 cup chorizo, cooked and crumbled
- 1/2 cup lettuce, shredded
- 1/4 cup tomato, sliced
- 1/4 cup pickled red onions
- Salsa (optional)

Instructions:

1. **Prepare the Tlayuda Base:**
   - Preheat your oven to 400°F (200°C). Place the tortillas on a baking sheet and bake for 5-7 minutes until crispy.
2. **Assemble the Tlayuda Pizza:**
   - Spread a thin layer of refried black beans on each crispy tortilla. Sprinkle with Oaxaca cheese and top with cooked chorizo.
3. **Finish and Serve:**
   - Return to the oven for 5 more minutes, or until the cheese is melted and bubbly.
   - Top with shredded lettuce, tomato slices, pickled red onions, and serve with salsa if desired.

Grilled Zucchini and Elote Salad

Ingredients:

- 2 zucchini, sliced into rounds
- 2 ears of corn, husked
- 1 tablespoon olive oil
- Salt and pepper to taste
- 1/4 cup fresh cilantro, chopped
- 1/4 cup crumbled queso fresco
- 1 tablespoon lime juice
- 1 tablespoon chili powder

Instructions:

1. **Grill the Vegetables:**
   - Preheat the grill to medium-high heat. Brush zucchini slices and corn with olive oil and season with salt and pepper.
   - Grill zucchini for 3-4 minutes per side, and grill the corn until charred, about 8-10 minutes.
2. **Assemble the Salad:**
   - Cut the kernels off the grilled corn and combine them with the grilled zucchini in a large bowl.
   - Add cilantro, queso fresco, lime juice, and chili powder. Toss to combine.
3. **Serve:**
   - Serve the salad warm or at room temperature.

Tamarind-Marinated Fish Filets

Ingredients:

- 4 fish filets (such as cod or halibut)
- 1/4 cup tamarind paste
- 2 tablespoons honey
- 1 tablespoon soy sauce
- 1 teaspoon ground cumin
- 1 teaspoon chili powder
- Salt and pepper to taste
- 1 tablespoon olive oil

Instructions:

1. **Prepare the Marinade:**
    - In a bowl, combine tamarind paste, honey, soy sauce, cumin, chili powder, salt, and pepper. Mix until smooth.
2. **Marinate the Fish:**
    - Place the fish filets in a shallow dish and pour the marinade over them. Let marinate for 30 minutes.
3. **Cook the Fish:**
    - Heat olive oil in a skillet over medium-high heat. Cook the fish filets for 3-4 minutes per side until cooked through and flaky.
4. **Serve:**
    - Serve the fish with rice or a side salad.

Cactus and Cheese Stuffed Arepas

Ingredients:

- 2 cups arepa flour
- 2 cups water
- 1 teaspoon salt
- 1 tablespoon olive oil
- 1 cup cooked and chopped cactus (nopales)
- 1/2 cup Oaxaca cheese, shredded
- 1/4 cup fresh cilantro, chopped

Instructions:

1. **Prepare the Arepas Dough:**
    - In a bowl, combine the arepa flour, water, and salt. Mix until a dough forms. Let rest for 5 minutes.
2. **Make the Stuffing:**
    - In a separate bowl, combine the cooked cactus, Oaxaca cheese, and cilantro.
3. **Shape and Cook the Arepas:**
    - Divide the dough into small balls. Flatten each ball into a patty and place a spoonful of the cactus and cheese mixture in the center. Seal the edges and form into a round shape.
    - Heat olive oil in a skillet over medium heat and cook the arepas for 4-5 minutes per side until golden brown and crispy.
4. **Serve:**
    - Serve the cactus and cheese stuffed arepas warm with salsa on the side.

Seared Scallops with Tomatillo Salsa

Ingredients:

- 12 large scallops, cleaned and patted dry
- Salt and pepper to taste
- 1 tablespoon olive oil
- 1/2 cup tomatillos, husked and chopped
- 1/4 cup fresh cilantro, chopped
- 1 tablespoon lime juice
- 1 small jalapeño, chopped (optional)

Instructions:

1. **Prepare the Salsa:**
    - In a blender, combine tomatillos, cilantro, lime juice, and jalapeño (if using). Blend until smooth.
2. **Cook the Scallops:**
    - Season the scallops with salt and pepper. Heat olive oil in a skillet over medium-high heat and sear the scallops for 2-3 minutes per side until golden brown.
3. **Serve:**
    - Spoon the tomatillo salsa onto plates and top with the seared scallops. Serve immediately.

Churro Cheesecake Bars

Ingredients:

- 1 package graham cracker crumbs
- 1/2 cup melted butter
- 1 package cream cheese, softened
- 1 cup sour cream
- 1/2 cup sugar
- 2 large eggs
- 1 teaspoon vanilla extract
- 1 teaspoon cinnamon
- 1/2 cup sugar (for topping)

Instructions:

1. **Prepare the Crust:**
    - Preheat the oven to 350°F (175°C). Combine graham cracker crumbs with melted butter. Press into the bottom of a baking dish.
2. **Make the Cheesecake Filling:**
    - In a bowl, beat the cream cheese with sour cream, sugar, eggs, and vanilla until smooth. Pour the mixture over the crust.
3. **Bake the Cheesecake:**
    - Bake for 25-30 minutes until the center is set.
4. **Make the Churro Topping:**
    - In a small bowl, mix cinnamon and sugar. Sprinkle this over the baked cheesecake bars.
5. **Serve:**
    - Let the cheesecake bars cool before slicing and serving.

Mexican Hot Chocolate Tart

Ingredients:

- 1 pre-made chocolate tart crust
- 1 1/2 cups heavy cream
- 8 oz Mexican chocolate, chopped
- 2 tablespoons sugar
- 1/2 teaspoon cinnamon
- 1/4 teaspoon chili powder (optional)
- 1 teaspoon vanilla extract
- Whipped cream for garnish

Instructions:

1. **Make the Filling:**
    - In a saucepan, heat the heavy cream over medium heat until simmering. Remove from heat and add chopped Mexican chocolate. Stir until smooth.
    - Stir in sugar, cinnamon, chili powder (if using), and vanilla extract.
2. **Fill the Tart:**
    - Pour the chocolate mixture into the pre-made tart crust. Refrigerate for at least 2 hours to set.
3. **Serve:**
    - Serve the tart chilled, topped with whipped cream.

Roasted Tomato and Guajillo Salsa

Ingredients:

- 4 medium tomatoes
- 2 dried guajillo chiles, seeds removed
- 1 small onion, quartered
- 2 cloves garlic, unpeeled
- 1 tablespoon olive oil
- 1 teaspoon ground cumin
- Salt to taste
- 1/4 cup fresh cilantro, chopped
- 1 tablespoon lime juice

Instructions:

1. **Roast the Vegetables:**
   - Preheat the oven to 400°F (200°C). Place the tomatoes, onion, and garlic on a baking sheet. Roast for 15-20 minutes until the vegetables are softened and slightly charred.
2. **Prepare the Guajillo Chiles:**
   - While the vegetables are roasting, place the dried guajillo chiles in a bowl and cover with hot water. Let them soak for about 10 minutes to soften.
3. **Blend the Salsa:**
   - In a blender, combine the roasted vegetables, soaked guajillo chiles, cumin, salt, cilantro, and lime juice. Blend until smooth. Taste and adjust seasoning if necessary.
4. **Serve:**
   - Serve the salsa with tortilla chips, tacos, or grilled meats.

Slow-Cooked Pork Pozole Verde

Ingredients:

- 2 lbs pork shoulder, cut into chunks
- 1 onion, quartered
- 3 cloves garlic, smashed
- 2 dried guajillo chiles, seeds removed
- 2 cups chicken broth
- 1 tablespoon olive oil
- 3 cups hominy, drained and rinsed
- 1/2 cup fresh cilantro, chopped
- 1 lime, cut into wedges
- 2 teaspoons oregano
- Salt and pepper to taste
- Sliced radishes and cabbage for garnish

Instructions:

1. **Cook the Pork:**
    - In a large pot, heat olive oil over medium-high heat. Brown the pork chunks in batches. Remove and set aside.
2. **Prepare the Broth:**
    - In the same pot, add the onion, garlic, and dried guajillo chiles. Toast for 2 minutes, then add the chicken broth and bring to a simmer. Once simmering, return the pork to the pot.
3. **Slow-Cook:**
    - Cover the pot and reduce the heat to low. Let the pork cook for 2-3 hours until it is tender and easily shreds with a fork.
4. **Add Hominy:**
    - Stir in the hominy, cilantro, oregano, and lime juice. Let cook for another 30 minutes. Adjust seasoning with salt and pepper.
5. **Serve:**
    - Ladle the pozole into bowls and garnish with radishes, cabbage, and additional lime wedges.

Chipotle Honey Glazed Salmon

Ingredients:

- 4 salmon fillets
- 2 tablespoons chipotle in adobo sauce, finely chopped
- 2 tablespoons honey
- 1 tablespoon olive oil
- 1 tablespoon lime juice
- Salt and pepper to taste
- Fresh cilantro for garnish

Instructions:

1. **Prepare the Glaze:**
   - In a small bowl, combine chipotle in adobo, honey, olive oil, lime juice, salt, and pepper. Stir until well combined.
2. **Cook the Salmon:**
   - Preheat a grill or skillet over medium-high heat. Brush the salmon fillets with the glaze and cook for 3-4 minutes per side, or until the salmon is cooked through and flakes easily with a fork.
3. **Serve:**
   - Garnish the salmon with fresh cilantro and serve with a side of rice or vegetables.

Poblano and Corn Fritters

Ingredients:

- 2 poblano peppers, roasted, peeled, and diced
- 1 cup corn kernels (fresh or frozen)
- 1/2 cup flour
- 1/2 teaspoon baking powder
- 1 teaspoon chili powder
- Salt and pepper to taste
- 2 large eggs
- 1/4 cup milk
- 1 tablespoon olive oil, for frying
- Fresh cilantro for garnish

Instructions:

1. **Prepare the Fritter Batter:**
   - In a large bowl, combine flour, baking powder, chili powder, salt, and pepper. Add the eggs and milk, and stir until smooth. Fold in the diced poblano peppers and corn.
2. **Fry the Fritters:**
   - Heat olive oil in a skillet over medium heat. Scoop spoonfuls of the batter into the hot oil and fry for 2-3 minutes per side until golden brown and crispy.
3. **Serve:**
   - Remove the fritters from the skillet and place them on a paper towel to drain. Garnish with fresh cilantro and serve with a side of salsa or dipping sauce.

Guacamole with Pomegranate Seeds

Ingredients:

- 3 ripe avocados, peeled and mashed
- 1/2 small onion, finely chopped
- 1 small tomato, diced
- 1 jalapeño, minced (optional)
- 1 tablespoon lime juice
- Salt and pepper to taste
- 1/2 cup pomegranate seeds

Instructions:

1. **Make the Guacamole:**
   - In a large bowl, combine mashed avocados, onion, tomato, jalapeño, lime juice, salt, and pepper. Mix until well combined.
2. **Add the Pomegranate:**
   - Gently fold in the pomegranate seeds.
3. **Serve:**
   - Serve the guacamole with tortilla chips or as a topping for tacos.

Mango Habanero Chicken Wings

Ingredients:

- 12 chicken wings, trimmed
- 1/2 cup mango puree
- 1 habanero pepper, seeds removed and finely chopped
- 1 tablespoon honey
- 1 tablespoon lime juice
- 1 tablespoon soy sauce
- Salt and pepper to taste
- Fresh cilantro for garnish

Instructions:

1. **Prepare the Marinade:**
   - In a bowl, combine mango puree, habanero pepper, honey, lime juice, soy sauce, salt, and pepper. Stir well.
2. **Marinate the Chicken:**
   - Toss the chicken wings in the marinade and let them marinate for at least 30 minutes.
3. **Cook the Wings:**
   - Preheat the grill or oven to 400°F (200°C). Grill the wings for 20-25 minutes or bake for 30 minutes, turning halfway, until they are crispy and cooked through.
4. **Serve:**
   - Garnish with fresh cilantro and serve with a cooling dip on the side, such as ranch or yogurt.

Chile Rellenos with Shrimp

Ingredients:

- 4 large poblano peppers
- 1 lb shrimp, peeled and deveined
- 1/2 cup cheese (queso fresco or Monterey Jack), grated
- 1 small onion, chopped
- 2 cloves garlic, minced
- 1/4 cup cilantro, chopped
- 1 tablespoon olive oil
- 2 eggs (separated)
- 1/4 cup flour
- Salt and pepper to taste
- Vegetable oil for frying
- Salsa for serving (optional)

Instructions:

1. **Roast the Poblano Peppers:**
    - Roast the poblanos over an open flame or on a baking sheet in a 400°F (200°C) oven until the skins are blackened. Place in a bowl, cover with a towel, and let steam for 10 minutes. Peel off the skins, cut a slit down the side, and remove the seeds.
2. **Prepare the Shrimp Filling:**
    - Heat olive oil in a pan over medium heat. Add the shrimp, onion, and garlic. Cook for 3-4 minutes until the shrimp turns pink. Remove from heat, stir in cilantro, and season with salt and pepper. Let the filling cool slightly.
3. **Stuff the Peppers:**
    - Stuff each poblano pepper with the shrimp mixture and grated cheese. Close the slit in each pepper.
4. **Batter and Fry:**
    - In a bowl, beat the egg whites until stiff peaks form. In a separate bowl, whisk the egg yolks with flour, salt, and pepper. Gently fold the egg whites into the yolk mixture. Dip the stuffed peppers into the batter and fry in hot oil for 2-3 minutes until golden brown. Drain on paper towels.
5. **Serve:**
    - Serve the chile rellenos with your favorite salsa or a drizzle of sour cream.

Black Bean and Goat Cheese Stuffed Peppers

Ingredients:

- 4 bell peppers, halved and seeded
- 1 can (15 oz) black beans, drained and rinsed
- 1/2 cup goat cheese, crumbled
- 1/2 cup corn kernels
- 1 small onion, diced
- 1 teaspoon cumin
- 1 teaspoon chili powder
- 1 tablespoon olive oil
- Salt and pepper to taste
- Fresh cilantro for garnish

Instructions:

1. **Prepare the Peppers:**
   - Preheat the oven to 375°F (190°C). Place the halved bell peppers on a baking dish and roast for 15-20 minutes, or until slightly tender.
2. **Prepare the Filling:**
   - Heat olive oil in a skillet over medium heat. Add the onion and cook until softened. Add the black beans, corn, cumin, chili powder, salt, and pepper. Stir to combine and cook for another 5 minutes.
3. **Stuff the Peppers:**
   - Stuff the roasted peppers with the black bean mixture. Top with crumbled goat cheese.
4. **Bake:**
   - Return the stuffed peppers to the oven and bake for an additional 10 minutes, or until the cheese is melted.
5. **Serve:**
   - Garnish with fresh cilantro and serve with a side of rice or salad.

Pulled Pork Enchilada Casserole

Ingredients:

- 2 cups cooked pulled pork
- 10 corn tortillas, cut into strips
- 2 cups red enchilada sauce
- 1 cup shredded cheddar cheese
- 1 cup shredded Monterey Jack cheese
- 1 small onion, diced
- 1/2 cup sour cream (optional, for serving)
- Fresh cilantro for garnish

Instructions:

1. **Prepare the Casserole:**
    - Preheat the oven to 350°F (175°C). In a large baking dish, layer the bottom with a few tortilla strips. Spread half of the pulled pork over the tortillas and drizzle with half of the enchilada sauce. Add a layer of cheese and top with more tortilla strips.
2. **Layer and Bake:**
    - Repeat the layering process with the remaining pulled pork, enchilada sauce, and cheese. Bake the casserole for 20-25 minutes, until the cheese is melted and bubbly.
3. **Serve:**
    - Garnish with diced onion, sour cream, and fresh cilantro. Serve with a side of rice or beans.

Spicy Jalapeño Margarita

Ingredients:

- 2 oz tequila
- 1 oz lime juice
- 1 oz triple sec
- 1/2 oz simple syrup
- 1/2 fresh jalapeño, sliced
- Salt for the rim
- Ice

Instructions:

1. **Prepare the Glass:**
   - Run a lime wedge around the rim of your glass and dip it into salt.
2. **Mix the Margarita:**
   - In a cocktail shaker, muddle the jalapeño slices. Add tequila, lime juice, triple sec, simple syrup, and ice. Shake well.
3. **Serve:**
   - Strain the margarita into the prepared glass and garnish with a lime wedge or additional jalapeño slices.

Hibiscus and Orange Agua Fresca

Ingredients:

- 1/2 cup dried hibiscus flowers
- 1 orange, juiced
- 4 cups water
- 2 tablespoons sugar (or to taste)
- Ice

Instructions:

1. **Make the Hibiscus Tea:**
    - Boil 2 cups of water and pour over the dried hibiscus flowers. Let it steep for about 10 minutes, then strain and discard the flowers.
2. **Mix the Agua Fresca:**
    - In a large pitcher, combine the hibiscus tea, orange juice, remaining water, and sugar. Stir until the sugar is dissolved.
3. **Serve:**
    - Serve over ice and garnish with orange slices.

Tequila Lime Cheesecake

Ingredients:

For the crust:

- 1 cup graham cracker crumbs
- 1/4 cup sugar
- 1/2 teaspoon ground cinnamon
- 1/4 cup melted butter

For the filling:

- 2 cups cream cheese, softened
- 1 cup sour cream
- 1/2 cup sugar
- 2 large eggs
- 2 tablespoons tequila
- Zest of 2 limes
- 1/4 cup lime juice

Instructions:

1. **Make the Crust:**
    - Preheat the oven to 325°F (160°C). In a bowl, combine graham cracker crumbs, sugar, cinnamon, and melted butter. Press the mixture into the bottom of a springform pan and bake for 8-10 minutes. Let it cool.
2. **Make the Filling:**
    - In a large mixing bowl, beat the cream cheese, sour cream, and sugar until smooth. Add the eggs one at a time, mixing well after each addition. Stir in tequila, lime zest, and lime juice.
3. **Bake the Cheesecake:**
    - Pour the filling over the cooled crust and bake for 45-50 minutes, or until the center is set. Let the cheesecake cool to room temperature, then refrigerate for at least 4 hours.
4. **Serve:**
    - Top with fresh lime slices or whipped cream and serve chilled.

www.ingramcontent.com/pod-product-compliance
Lightning Source LLC
LaVergne TN
LVHW081320060526
838201LV00055B/2390